QUESTIONS THAT CREATE CLARITY

A RELATIONSHIP-DRIVEN GUIDE TO NEW HOME SALES

RYAN ROTEN

CONTENTS

Questions That Create Clarity

A Relationship-Driven Guide to New Home Sales

To my wife, Vanessa, and our six incredible children. Thank you for your love, patience, and constant encouragement.

Everything meaningful in my life begins with you.

FOREWORD

WHY THIS BOOK EXISTS

When I first started in new home sales, I thought success came down to personality and product knowledge—talk well, know your stuff, and people will buy. But over time, I learned that those things only take you so far. The true difference between good and great salespeople isn't in what they know—it's in how they *think*.

Mindset is everything in this business.

It shapes how we show up, how we connect, and how we handle the ups and downs that come with this career. This book was born from nearly two decades of lessons—the tough seasons when traffic was slow, the record-breaking months that tested my systems, and the hundreds of families I've had the privilege to help along the way.

If you're in new home sales—whether you're brand new or a seasoned pro—my goal is to give you a practical, real-world guide you can use every day. Not theory. Not fluff. Just the truths that actually work in this business.

Let's start with the foundation of it all—the mindset that turns an average salesperson into a trusted advisor.

1

MINDSET AND APPROACH
UNDERSTANDING THE ROLE OF A
NEW HOME SALES PROFESSIONAL

The Right Mindset Sets the Tone

New home sales is not a job—it's a mission that requires purpose and patience. Every conversation, every tour, and every handshake has the potential to shape someone's life. That's a level of impact that deserves intention.

The way you think before a buyer ever walks through the door largely determines how that interaction will unfold. The best sales professionals don't wait for the right buyer to make their day better—they decide, before the day begins, that it's going to be a great one.

I've seen talented people walk into their models with energy that says, *"I hope someone comes in today."* And I've seen top producers walk in with energy that says, *"Someone's coming in today—and when they do, I'm ready."*

That small difference in mindset doesn't just change results—it changes the entire experience. The room feels different. The tone shifts. Confidence becomes contagious.

One phrase changed how I approach every day:

"Act as if every room you walk into, God sent you there for a purpose."

Mindset Reset

Before you unlock your model home each morning, take a moment and say to yourself:

"Today, someone's life could change—and I'll be part of it."

That ten second reset shifts your focus from waiting for business to being ready for it.

Traffic, market conditions, and interest rates are outside of your control. Your energy, consistency, and approach are not.

The right mindset doesn't guarantee a sale every day—but it does guarantee something better. Every person who walks through your door feels seen, valued, and remembered. That's what separates a salesperson from a professional.

Serving Before Selling

When a buyer walks into your model home, they're not simply searching for four walls and a roof—they're looking for a way to improve their life.

Most of the time, they don't know exactly what that means yet. They may think it's a bigger kitchen or another bedroom, but underneath that is a hope for something more—peace, comfort, safety, pride, or space to grow. Your job is to uncover that deeper reason.

Trust is the true currency of new-home sales, but buyers don't walk in already trusting you. They've been advertised to, pressured, or ignored elsewhere—so you have to earn it. And you don't earn trust by talking; you earn it by listening.

One couple I met years ago taught me this better than any training ever could. They walked in saying they "just wanted to look." Instead of launching into incentives or features they hadn't asked about, I let them know that it was completely okay to look around and that I'd be there if any questions came up.

I let them walk down the hallway and I casually asked if I could get them some water. That small gesture helped open the door to trust. After a bit of light conversation, I learned they were actually in the market for a new home—they just didn't know where to start.

That's when I asked a simple but powerful question:

"What's prompting the move right now?"

The wife paused, looked at her husband, and said quietly, *"We've been caring for my mother, and she's coming to live with us. We need space that works for everyone."*

In that moment, it wasn't about selling a house anymore—it was about helping them find a home that could support a new chapter of life. Once I understood that, the entire conversation changed.

That's what *serving before selling* really means. You stop seeing visitors as leads and start seeing them as people with stories. And when people feel understood, they naturally start to trust you.

Pro Tip:

When a buyer says, *"We're just looking,"* that's not a brush-off—it's a defense mechanism.

Respond with warmth instead of pressure:
"Perfect—this is a great place to start. Is there anything specific you were hoping to see while you're out today?"

A gentle question like that turns a cold introduction into an open conversation—and that's where real sales begin.

Once you commit to serving first, you need a framework that keeps your conversations focused and intentional. Without one, even the best intentions can turn into scattered conversations or missed opportunities.

The 3 C's of Service

Great salespeople don't just sell—they *serve*.

Over the years, I've learned that success in this business isn't about memorizing scripts or mastering every closing line. It's about living by a simple framework I call **The 3 C's of Service**—the foundation for every great sales interaction:

Curiosity

Ask with genuine interest. Don't assume you already know their story—draw it out. Be more focused on learning than persuading. Curiosity signals care, and people open up when they feel you're truly interested.

Connection

Listen for emotion, not just logistics. When someone tells you they "need another bedroom," what they might really be saying is, "We need peace and space." Your job is to listen *beneath* the surface and identify what actually matters to them.

Clarity

Before offering solutions, summarize what you've heard. When buyers hear their own priorities reflected back to them, they feel seen—and that feeling builds trust faster than any sales tactic ever could.

When you approach discovery this way, the buyer doesn't feel sold —they feel guided. And that's the difference between a one-time transaction and a long-term relationship.

Another way to think about it is this: your appointment should flow like a story, not a presentation. Every strong sales experience naturally moves through five stages:

Greeting → Discovery → Qualification → Showing → Closing.

Each stage has a purpose. When you move through them with curiosity and care, the buyer feels like the process is unfolding *with* them—not *at* them.

Connection Cue:
Try saying, *"What's inspiring this move for you?"* instead of *"Why are you moving?"*

"Why" can feel interrogative and put people on the defensive; "What's inspiring…" invites them to share. That simple shift turns short, surface answers into meaningful stories—and those stories become the foundation of your recommendations later.

Personal Note:

After every appointment, take five minutes to write down what you learned—before you check your email, before you greet the next person. The more detailed your notes, the more prepared "future you" will be when that buyer returns.

Buyers often tell me, "We decided to work with you because you actually remembered what we said." That isn't a memory trick— it's discipline. It's caring enough to document their story.

Most of the families I've helped over the years didn't choose me because I had the best incentives or flashiest model home. They chose me because they could feel that I genuinely cared about finding the right home for their family.

In new home sales, serving comes before selling—and ironically, that's what makes selling easier.

Balancing Emotion and Logic

Buying a home is both emotional and logical—a head-and-heart decision that touches nearly every area of a family's life.

They're picturing birthdays, holidays, and quiet mornings. They're imagining their kids growing up in the space and routines forming over time. At the same time, they're running calculations in their heads—down payment, monthly payment, taxes, interest rates, and whether this is *the right time*.

Your role is to help them balance both worlds: to honor the emotion that brought them in, while providing the clarity and confidence to move forward wisely.

I've seen this dynamic play out countless times. A couple walks in with excitement and vision, but somewhere between the kitchen island and the financing discussion, their energy shifts. They stop smiling. Their tone changes. The emotion that carried them in gets overtaken by fear or doubt.

That's exactly what happened with one couple I met in 2022. They were relocating from out of state and were genuinely excited about the community and the floor plan. But once we started talking about the numbers, everything slowed down.

Instead of pushing, I paused and said,

"This is a big decision—let's *slow down*. What's holding you back right now?"

That question opened the door. They explained they had just sold their previous home and were worried about buying again with interest rates rising. It wasn't the payment that scared them — it was the fear of timing it wrong.

As we talked, it became clear they weren't afraid of the payment—they were afraid of regret.

Once we reframed the conversation around how long they planned to live there, what stability meant to them, and what their long-term goals really were, everything shifted. They realized that even if rates moved slightly, their long-term gain in quality of life outweighed the short-term uncertainty.

Pro Tip:
When a buyer hesitates, don't rush to fill the silence with more information—that's usually when the truth is about to surface.

Try asking:

• "What's holding you back right now?"

• "What's making this decision feel heavy?"

• "What's the one thing you wish you were sure about?"

These versions sound empathetic, not scripted—and they invite honesty.

Then listen carefully. The first answer they give is rarely the real one. If you stay quiet just a moment longer, they'll tell you what's actually standing in their way.

When you guide buyers this way, you become more than a salesperson, you become a trusted advisor helping them find clarity in one of life's biggest crossroads.

The Emotion–Logic Spectrum

Every buyer lands somewhere on a spectrum between emotion and logic.

Your job is to identify where they are and speak their language.

Emotional Buyers

Emotional Buyers lead with feeling—excitement, lifestyle, imagined family moments. You'll hear things like, "I can just see us hosting Christmas here." Help them visualize and paint vivid pictures that let them see their future:

"Imagine your kids running down this hallway on Christmas morning."

Analytical Buyers

Analytical buyers lead with data—square footage, pricing, comparisons, and efficiency. They'll ask questions like, "What's the cost per square foot?" or "How does this compare to the builder across the street?"

Serve them with:

- Clear numbers
- Organized options
- Side-by-side comparisons

Balanced Buyers

Balanced Buyers use both heart and head. They want to feel confident *and* inspired.

Affirm their emotion, then support it with logic:

"You love the natural light—and it also keeps your energy bills lower all year."

Once you learn which side a buyer leans toward, adjust your pace, tone, and emphasis accordingly.

When Logic Overpowers Emotion

Some buyers bring spreadsheets, comparison charts, and calculators to every appointment. They can analyze the joy right out of the experience.

When that happens, gently redirect them back to why they started.

I'll often say,

"Let's zoom out for a second and remember what made this home feel right for your family in the first place. We've already walked through the numbers together, and they made sense for you. Has anything changed since then?"

That question reframes the moment. It reminds buyers they're not choosing a spreadsheet—they're choosing their future lifestyle.

When Emotion Overpowers Logic

Other buyers fall in love quickly. The excitement is real—until reality catches up.

If a home stretches their comfort zone, I slow the moment down with empathy:

"I can see how much you love this plan. Let's make sure it fits where you want to be financially, too. The last thing I want is for you to feel stress instead of joy when you move in."

Emotion drives action, but logic sustains confidence. When both align, cancellations drop and satisfaction rises.

🪨 The "Feel–Think–Do" Model

Feel: Connect with what motivated them to walk in.
Think: Provide clarity, numbers, and perspective.
Do: Guide them toward confident action.

When buyers feel safe in both emotion and reason, they move forward faster—and with fewer regrets.

Great salespeople aren't manipulative—they're interpreters. They translate emotion into logical comfort, and logic into emotional reassurance.

When you learn to balance those two languages, your presentations stop feeling like pitches—and start feeling like teamwork.

The ability to serve well, ask better questions, and balance emotion with logic doesn't happen by accident. It starts with mindset—how you see your role, how you show up each day, and how intentionally you approach every conversation. When your mindset is aligned, everything else in the sales process becomes clearer and more natural.

But mindset alone isn't enough.

The habits you build, the consistency you maintain, and the resilience you develop during slow seasons are what turn good intentions into lasting results. That's where professionalism is forged—not in the easy wins, but in the daily disciplines that shape who you become in this business.

Closing Thoughts

The right mindset doesn't always make sales easier—it makes *you* stronger.

When you commit to serving before selling, listening before talking, and guiding before pushing, you create an experience buyers can feel. You stop chasing outcomes and start building trust. And trust, when nurtured consistently, always produces results.

You're not just selling homes.

You're helping families make one of the most important decisions of their lives. That responsibility deserves intention, patience, and care—even on the days when traffic is slow, deals fall apart, or motivation feels thin.

If you wake up each morning grounded in gratitude, curiosity, and a commitment to growth, success will find you in time. Not because you chased it, but because you became the kind of professional people want to work with.

With the right mindset established, the next step is learning how to show up consistently—day after day, season after season—no matter what the market is doing.

Reflection

- What is one mindset shift you can make starting tomorrow?
- Which of the 3 C's—Curiosity, Connection, or Clarity—do you most need to strengthen right now?
- On a scale of 1–10, how consistent have you been this month in how you show up for buyers?

_____

_____

_____

_____

_____

_____

_____

_____

_____

_____

_____

Mindset and Approach

_____

_____

_____

_____

_____

_____

_____

_____

_____

_____

_____

_____

_____

_____

_____

_____

_____

_____

_____

_____

2

CONSISTENCY, RESILIENCE, AND PROFESSIONAL GROWTH
CONSISTENCY BUILDS CONFIDENCE

I f there's one thing I've learned over nearly two decades in sales, it's that consistency beats talent every time.

You don't have to be the flashiest talker or the most charismatic personality to succeed in new-home sales—you just have to show up the same way, every day.

Consistency builds confidence, and confidence builds trust.

Buyers don't trust words; they trust patterns.

They watch whether you call when you said you would, whether you remember what mattered to them, and whether your follow-through matches your promises.

Practice Builds Predictability

Most people hate role-playing, but it's the fastest way to sharpen your craft.

If you can't bring yourself to role-play with someone else, do it with yourself.

Stand in front of a mirror. Record your greeting and listen to it back.

Watch your posture, tone, and timing.

The goal isn't perfection—it's awareness.

Every time you rehearse, you reduce the chance of freezing in front of a real buyer.

And here's the truth: the top performers in any field practice far more than they perform.

Follow-Through Is Your Silent Closer

I still remember the first time consistency clicked for me.

A couple had visited the model the previous weekend. I promised to follow up on Tuesday afternoon with updated lot availability. Even though I didn't have new information yet, I called exactly when I said I would.

The husband answered and laughed, "You actually called when you said you would? Nobody does that anymore."

That small, simple act built instant credibility. It didn't close the sale that day, but two weeks later, they signed a contract.

> **Pro Tip:**
> Follow-through is your silent closer.
> Do what you say you'll do — especially when there's
> nothing in it for you yet.

The Consistency Compass

Top performers don't rely on motivation — they rely on systems.

Motivation gets you started; systems keep you going when you're tired, busy, or discouraged.

Here's the **Consistency Compass** I personally live by — four daily habits that compound results over time:

1. **Show Up Early:** Being ready before your first appointment isn't about the clock — it's about mindset. Walking in early lets you prepare the model, review notes, and set your tone for the day.

2. **Follow Up Daily:** Even on busy days, never leave without sending at least three personalized follow-ups. They don't need to be long — just thoughtful. A quick text like, "Hey, I was thinking about that corner lot you liked — it's still available," goes further than any email blast.

3. **Review and Reflect:** Before you head home, review your conversations. Ask yourself: *Who connected? Who stalled? What's next?* Then write it down. It sharpens your instincts over time.

4. **Prepare Tomorrow, Tonight:** End each day by

previewing tomorrow. Know who's coming, what they liked, and how you can make their visit personal.

✓ The 1% Rule

Get 1% better every day.
You won't notice it right away, but over a year, that's a *37x improvement*. I promise the math works out!
The pros don't chase perfection — they chase progress.

Honesty Creates Ease

There's a saying I live by:

"If you don't lie, you don't have to remember anything."

When your communication is truthful, you never scramble to recall what you told someone. Integrity simplifies everything — and simplicity builds peace of mind.

Consistency Creates Predictability

When you operate from a rhythm, buyers sense it.

They feel you're organized, steady, and trustworthy.

That predictability lowers stress for everyone.

Realtors trust you more. Construction managers communicate better.

And you stop burning mental energy worrying about what's next — because your system already knows.

One of the things I admire about my company is that our reputation for quality and consistency runs deep — not just in our product, but in how we communicate. We truly believe we're the best.

As sales professionals, we should mirror that same dependability personally.

You're not just representing a builder — you're representing a brand that buyers will remember long after closing.

For most, you are the first face of that brand they'll ever meet.

🏷 The Consistency Checkup

At the end of every week, ask yourself three questions:
Did I keep every promise I made to a buyer?
Did I follow up with everyone who deserved a call or text?
Did I treat every visitor as if they were my only customer that day?
If you can answer "yes" to all three, you're not just consistent — you're dependable.

Consistency isn't flashy. It doesn't trend online or win awards overnight. But it builds momentum — and momentum builds everything else. Stay consistent long enough, and your results will look like luck to everyone else.

Resilience in a Cyclical Industry

If you've been in new-home sales long enough, you know the market moves in waves. There are seasons when you can't keep up

— contracts flying, phones buzzing, buyers lining up — and there are seasons when the model door doesn't open for days, and you wonder if you'll ever sell another home.

This is a cyclical business. It always has been.

And resilience — not hype, not luck, not even perfect timing — is what determines who lasts and who burns out.

I've seen it time and time again. The same salesperson who's unstoppable during boom times can crumble when things slow down. They lose focus, lose faith, and start blaming interest rates, the builder, or "the market."

But here's the truth: the best don't panic — they **pivot.**

> **Mindset Reset:**
> When traffic slows, don't ask, "Where is everyone?"
> Ask, "What can I control right now that others aren't doing?"

Every Cycle Tests You Differently

When the market is hot, your challenge is managing volume — keeping communication clear, staying organized, and protecting your energy.

When the market slows, your challenge is maintaining momentum — staying visible, keeping your name out there, and sharpening your process.

I still remember the shift after the COVID boom. For a stretch, it felt like sales would never stop — I had one month where I sold sixteen homes, and the builder actually had to pause sales so construction could catch up. 2022 and 2023 were incredible years.

But by early 2025, the faucet turned off almost overnight. Traffic slowed. The excitement changed.

Instead of panicking, I went back to the basics: follow-up, outreach, Realtor connections, and every buyer who'd once said "not yet."

That slower season became one of the best lead-building stretches of my career. By the time momentum returned, I already had a warm list while others were just restarting theirs.

That's the power of resilience: it turns waiting seasons into planting seasons.

> **Pro Tip:**
> Slow markets don't destroy your business — they reveal your discipline.

How to Build "Pressure-Tested" Confidence

Confidence in this industry isn't about pretending everything's fine — it's about staying focused when everything's uncertain.

The professionals who rise through downturns are the ones who keep doing the right things, even when those things don't produce instant results.

Here's how I define *pressure-tested confidence:*

1. **Perspective over Panic:** Remember, every market cycle ends. Focus on what lasts — your habits, relationships, and reputation.
2. **Action over Anxiety:** When things slow down, increase your output. Make more calls, send more videos, host more tours. Action beats fear.
3. **Gratitude over Grumbling:** Gratitude keeps you grounded. Ask yourself, "What am I *thankful* for right now?" The people who stay thankful in the valley are the ones flooded with opportunity on the next rise.

✓ The "Downtime Advantage"

Use slow seasons to master things that never lose value:
Know every lot, floor, and feature in your community.
Refresh your CRM with personalized notes and next step reminders.
Study interest rate programs and financing tools.
Build and strengthen relationships with Realtors and lenders.
When everyone else is waiting for business, you're preparing for it.

Play the Long Game

Resilient sales professionals understand that a career is built over years, not months.

They don't let short-term conditions define their long-term mindset.

Every season — even the tough ones — is shaping you into the kind of professional who can weather anything.

When I look back at my own career, my biggest growth didn't happen during the easy seasons — it happened when things were uncertain.

Those were the times I learned how to control what I could, let go of what I couldn't, and trust that the effort I put in today would pay off down the road.

Because in this business, it always does.

🥄 The 90-Day Rule

Whatever you do today will show up in your results about 90 days from now.
Don't judge your week by just how many contracts you wrote — also judge it by how many people you connected with.

Resilience isn't about being unshakable. It's about staying in motion when everyone else freezes.

The market will always shift, but if your mindset and your effort stay consistent, you'll always find a way to win — no matter the season.

Professionalism and Personal Growth

New home sales isn't a job you master once — it's a craft you refine for life.

The best professionals never stop learning, even when they're at the top of their game. They treat every appointment as a chance to improve, every challenge as a classroom, and every customer as a mirror showing them where they can grow.

Professionalism in this industry goes far beyond a nice outfit and a clean desk.

It's about **character**, **consistency**, and **care** — how you act and treat people when no one's watching, how you follow through on promises, and how you handle yourself when things don't go your way.

> **Pro Tip:**
> Professionalism is how you behave when the sale doesn't go through.

You Are Your Brand

Whether you work for a builder, brokerage, or yourself, *you* are the brand people remember.

Buyers might forget the floor plan names or the price per square foot — but they will never forget how you made them feel, good or bad.

If you're kind, knowledgeable, and dependable, they'll share your name with friends.

If you're dismissive, disorganized, or defensive, they'll talk about that too. Which one of those happens is up to you.

Every interaction either builds or breaks your reputation.

That's why every handshake, email, and walk-through matters. When you walk into your model each morning, remember: you're not just representing your builder — you're representing you.

For me, that means bringing my faith, my family, and my full self to work each day. No shortcuts. No excuses. No "good enough." Your name is your business card — even off the clock.

🖥 The Brand You Build
Ask yourself:
How do people describe me when I'm not around?
Would I hire myself to sell my own home?
Do my actions reflect my values every day?
If the answers make you proud, you're building the right brand.

Stay Teachable

The moment you think you've "arrived," you stop growing.

The top sales professionals I know — the ones who truly impact families — all share one trait: they stay teachable.

They read. They take notes. They seek feedback.

Not because they're insecure, but because they're humble enough to know there's always more to learn.

I still take notes when I listen to speakers like **Jeff Shore**. I still evaluate each closing and ask what I could've done better.

It's not self-criticism — it's self-awareness.

The second you stop evaluating your process, your process stops evolving.

The Growth Formula
Awareness + Action = Advancement.
You can't grow from what you ignore or refuse to acknowledge, and awareness means nothing without follow-through.

Guard Your Energy and Integrity

Professional growth also means protecting what fuels your performance — your mindset, your health, and your integrity.

Burnout and cynicism are silent killers in this business. They sneak in when you're overworked, under-rested, or chasing the wrong definition of success.

Guard your mornings. Protect your peace. Take care of your family and your faith before the day takes over.

And when challenges come — tough buyers, missed goals, or slow months — Respond Intentionally, don't react emotionally.

How you carry yourself under pressure is the true measure of professionalism.

Mindset Reminder:
You can't pour into others if your own cup is empty.

Commitment Beyond the Sale

Every closing is a finish line for the buyer, but it's just the next checkpoint for you.

Professionalism means following through after the contract — checking in after move-in to ensure satisfaction, solving problems, and staying available.

That's what separates salespeople from *advisors*.

The Long Game
Lead with *integrity*.
Learn without *ego*.
Serve without *conditions*.
That's how you build a career that lasts decades, not just seasons.

Closing Thoughts

The right mindset doesn't always make sales easier — it makes *you* stronger.

If you wake up every morning with gratitude, curiosity, and commitment to growth, success will always find you.

You're not just selling homes.

You're helping people build their lives — and that's a purpose worth showing up for every single day.

With the right mindset established, the next step is learning how to connect — to truly understand what buyers need and why they've come to you.

✎ Reflection

- What's one daily mindset shift you can make starting tomorrow?
- Which of the 3 C's do you most need to strengthen right now?
- How consistent are you this month on a scale of 1–10?

_____

_____

_____

_____

_____

_____

_____

_____

_____

_____

_____

_____

_____

_____

_____

_____

_____

_____

_____

_____

_____

_____

_____

_____

_____

_____

_____

_____

_____

3

THE POWER OF DISCOVERY AND CONNECTION

Discovery is more than asking questions — it's about connection.

I n new home sales, the best conversations don't feel scripted; they flow naturally, helping the buyer feel understood while giving you the insight to find their perfect home.

The goal is not to "sell" right away, but to *discover* — to truly listen, understand, and guide.

Because when a buyer feels heard, they stop seeing you as a salesperson... and start seeing you as a trusted advisor.

> **☺ Pro Tip:**
> The fastest way to earn trust is to *make the buyer the hero of the conversation.*
> Let them do most of the talking — your questions should simply guide their story.

The First Impression Matters

Buyers form an opinion about you long before they sit down at your desk.

From the moment they walk through the door, they're absorbing everything — your tone, your energy, your body language, and even how prepared you look.

I always start with something warm and human.

Something that immediately shifts the tone from *sales pitch* to *real conversation.*

☺ Possible Opening Lines

Here are a few go-to openers that start conversations instead of sales pitches:

- "Hey there — welcome in! What part of town are you coming from today?"
- "Good to see you! I'm so glad you stopped in — was it an easy drive over?"

- "Hey guys! I was just grabbing some coffee — you're right on time."

These simple openings lower walls. They're disarming, conversational, and authentic.

People can *feel* authenticity. And that first connection sets the tone for everything that follows.

📖 The 7-Second Rule
Studies show people form a first impression within **seven seconds**.
Your energy matters more than your words.
Smile. Be present. And most importantly, *be real.*

Becoming "Coffee-Worthy"

I'm not a coffee drinker myself, but sales trainer Jeff Shore once said, *"You want to be coffee-worthy."*

That line stuck with me. It's the perfect way to describe what our discovery conversations should feel like.

Your goal in discovery is to become *coffee-worthy* — the kind of person a buyer would happily sit down with over a cup of coffee, just because they enjoy talking to you.

That level of comfort only comes when the interaction feels **conversational**, not **transactional**.

Ask open-ended questions. Listen without interrupting.

And respond in a way that shows you're engaged in their answers. Show genuine curiosity about their story.

If a buyer says, *"We just need more space,"* don't stop there.

Say, *"Got it — what's creating that need for more space right now?"*

or

"I want to make sure I understand — what's missing in your current home that's creating that need?"

Every answer they give is an opportunity to uncover the *story behind the move* — which is often more important than the specs of the home.

● Coffee-Worthy Questions:
"What's inspiring the move right now?"
"What's your current home missing?"
"Why do you feel your current home doesn't fit your needs anymore?"
These questions build trust faster than any feature sheet ever could.

Reading the Buyer's Energy

Every buyer walks in carrying a unique emotional state.

Some are excited, ready to talk about everything they've researched. Others are cautious, quiet, and prefer to take things in slowly.

Your role is to match the buyer's energy. Some people describe this as "mirroring," but what I mean is something more natural and more human.

If a buyer walks in with high energy, ride that wave. Laugh with them. Engage. Celebrate the excitement they're bringing into the room.

If they're more reserved, slow down your pace. Give them space. Let them warm up on their own terms.

Sometimes this even shows up in small, unconscious ways like posture, body language, or how relaxed someone appears. When you naturally align with that rhythm, buyers feel more comfortable without knowing why.

This isn't about copying exact behavior or forcing rapport. It's emotional adaptability and it's one of the most underrated skills in sales.

Pro Tip:
Never outtalk a quiet buyer.
When you fill the silence too quickly, you take away their thinking time — and thinking time is buying time.

Digging Deeper to Discover True Needs

Buyers often tell you what they *think* they want — but your job is to help them discover what they *actually* need.

When someone says, *"We just need a bigger kitchen,"* it's rarely about the kitchen itself.

It might mean they host family dinners, or that their old layout never allowed them to cook together.

Ask:

"What about your current kitchen isn't working?"

"How do you imagine using your new one differently?"

These follow-ups bring emotion and purpose into the conversation — and that's where clarity lives.

The 3 Layers of Discovery

Surface: What they say ("We need more space.")
Structure: What they mean ("Our kids are sharing a room.")
Story: Why it matters ("We want them to feel independent.")
Your goal is to reach the *story* layer — that's where emotion and motivation connect.

Avoiding Common Traps

Even experienced sales professionals fall into these discovery traps:

1. **Assuming you already know the answer.**
   - Don't fill in blanks — ask for clarity instead.
2. **Talking too much about features too early.**

- ○ Focus on *people*, not *product*, in the first half of the appointment.
3. **Ignoring nonverbal cues.**
   - ○ Watch how buyers react to what you show — the truth is often in the body language.

Discovery isn't about dominating the conversation; it's about directing it with curiosity.

Pro Tip:
If you're the one talking more than 60% of the time, you're not discovering — you're pitching.

Capturing the Details that Matter

Taking notes during a buyer conversation can be just as important as asking the right questions.

For buyers who share a lot of details, it can help to ask:

"Do you mind if I take a few notes while we talk? I want to make sure I capture everything that's important to you."

It shows that you're **actively listening**, and it helps you remember the small details that often make or break a sale.

Detailed note-taking has saved the day countless times.

I once worked with a couple who had very specific requirements: the **kitchen had to face east** for morning light, and the **primary suite needed to sit on the southwest corner** for sunset views.

They'd worked with several agents before, but no one had really *heard* them.

By taking detailed notes and confirming each point, I was able to pinpoint a home that checked every box — and they wrote the contract two days later.

Sometimes it's not about how many homes you show; it's about how well you listen.

Real-Life Example: Matching the Home to the Buyer

A couple once told me they needed "space for homeschooling."

I immediately pictured a large upstairs game room with built-ins and extra lighting.

But when I showed them that plan, they said, *"It feels too big."*

That's when I realized what they *really* wanted wasn't more square footage — it was *better use* of space.

We found a home with a cozy loft just off the kids' bedrooms — compact, practical, and perfectly functional for their needs.

They wrote the contract that day.

The takeaway? Discovery isn't about guessing right; it's about asking until the right answer reveals itself.

✓ **The Discovery Formula**
Curiosity + Listening + Patience = Clarity.
You don't need all the answers. You just need to care
enough to find them.

Reflection – Turning Listening into Leadership

Your goal in every discovery conversation is connection — not
control.

When buyers feel truly heard, they'll trust you to guide them.

That trust turns curiosity into clarity, and clarity into contracts.

In a world full of sales noise, the person who listens best wins.

_____

_____

_____

_____

_____

_____

_____

_____

4

THE QUESTIONS THAT CREATE CLARITY

GREAT QUESTIONS CLARIFY, CONFIRM, AND CONNECT

G reat questions are the most powerful tool in sales — yet they're also the most underused.

Too many sales professionals think their job is to have the best answers, when in reality, their job is to ask the *best questions*.

Questions guide the buyer's thinking, uncover their motivation, and lead them to decisions they feel confident about.

They turn confusion into clarity — and clarity is what closes deals.

> **Pro Tip:**
> When you ask better questions, you don't have to "close" people — they close themselves.

Why Great Questions Matter

In new home sales, you're not selling just a product — you're helping people make one of the biggest life decisions they'll ever face.

And the only way to truly help is to understand what matters most to them.

Questions unlock that understanding.

They reveal priorities, pain points, and emotional triggers that a buyer might not even be consciously aware of.

For example, a simple, "What's most important to you in your next home?" might sound basic — but when you let them talk long enough, they'll tell you *everything* you need to know to earn their trust.

> The 3 Purposes of Great Questions
> **Clarify** what the buyer values most.
> **Confirm** that you understand their needs.
> **Connect** emotionally to their motivation for moving.

Understanding the Buyer's Budget

Money conversations are where a lot of salespeople freeze up — but they don't have to.

Handled correctly, these questions build *trust,* not tension.

Instead of asking, *"What's your budget?"* — which can sound transactional — try:

"What price range feels most comfortable for you?"

"If this home checked every box, how far could you stretch?"

"Have you been pre-approved yet?" *(If yes, follow with)* "Perfect! What number are you hoping to stay close to?"

These questions lower defenses and invite honesty.

They also show that you care about *fit,* not just a sale.

And when you know their range early, you can tailor your presentation to show homes that align with both their dreams *and* their reality.

If you're comfortable doing so, you can even help buyers visualize what their total payment might look like — breaking it down by **P&I, taxes, insurance, PMI, and any community fees.**

When you help buyers understand the full picture, you turn a stressful conversation into an empowering one. If you do not feel comfortable, get with a Loan Officer you trust and get comfortable. Learn how to use a Mortgage calculator and be able to use it in front of the customer. This will put a lot of trust in you because it helps them see that you know what you are doing and talking about.

> **Pro Tip:**
> Budget questions aren't about numbers — they're about *comfort and confidence.*
> People may hesitate at prices, but they'll move forward when they feel understood.

Timing and Motivation

If there's one question every sales professional should ask in the first five minutes, it's this one:

"How soon are you hoping to be in your new home?"

That one question unlocks *urgency, motivation, and emotional context.*

If their lease is up soon, you've got a time-driven buyer.

If they say "sometime next year," you've got a relationship-driven buyer who needs nurturing.

If they don't have a great answer for you, follow up with:

"If everything lined up perfectly, and the stars aligned, when would the move be?"

You invite them to dream a little — which softens the conversational tone and reveals what "perfect" really looks like to them. Now you can position your next steps naturally.

⏱ Timing Translates to Motivation

30–90 days: Solution seekers. They're ready — just need clarity.

3–6 months: Explorers. Build trust and follow up regularly.

6+ months: Relationship growers. Stay present and consistent.

Schools, Lifestyle, and Priorities

Every buyer is motivated by something different — and part of your role is learning what that is *for them.*

If they mention school-age kids, school districts can become an emotional topic.

If they're retirees, lifestyle and convenience might take center stage.

Ask about what matters beyond the floor plan:

"Tell me a little about what kind of community you're hoping to find."

"What's your favorite thing to do when you're just hanging out at home?"

When you ask lifestyle questions, you stop sounding like a salesperson — and start sounding like someone helping them design their next chapter.

Because that's who you are.

⌂ The Lifestyle Lens
Every floor plan tells a story.
Your job is to match the *story* to the *family*.

Adapting to Your Market

Not every neighborhood sells itself — and that's not a bad thing. It's actually a great opportunity for the professional who can set themselves and their company apart from the competition.

Some communities thrive on location and amenities, while others lean on builder quality, design, or financing programs.

The best salespeople don't just memorize features — they adapt their *questions* to match what their market values most.

For example:

- **Luxury market:** "What details are most important in your next home — design, finishes, flow, or a combination of those?"
- **Value-driven market:** "What's most important to you — payment comfort, square footage, or location?"

The same question asked the *right way* can change your entire outcome.

⋯ Pro Tip:
Don't just tailor your presentation — tailor your *questions*.

Handling Vague Answers

When a buyer gives you a vague answer like, *"We just need more space,"* that's your cue to dig deeper.

"What about your current home isn't working anymore?"

"How do you imagine using the extra space?"

These aren't just follow-ups — they're emotional clarifiers.

They turn surface wants into meaningful needs.

The "Why Behind the Why"
What do they want?
Why do they want it?
Why does *that* matter?
The third "why" is where motivation — and the sale — live.

The Catch & Release Method

Sometimes, discovery takes patience. If a buyer isn't opening up right away, you can't force it — you have to earn it.

Here's how it usually looks for me:

A buyer walks in. I greet them warmly:

"Hey there — how are you folks doing today?"

If they're standoffish and brush me off with a version of "We're just looking," I'll smile and reply,

49

"No problem at all — take your time looking around. Is there anything specific you're hoping to see while you're out today?"

Most say no, so I back off.

"Very cool! I'll be hiding in this office over here if any questions come up."

After a short pause, I'll casually ask,

"Would any of you like a water while you look around?"

That small gesture reopens the door — and about 25% of the time, it sparks real conversation.

For those who still stay quiet, I'll ask,

"Do you mind if I check in after about 5–10 minutes, just in case something comes up?"

Most say yes, which gives me permission to re-engage naturally later.

The point is: patience earns trust. Discovery can't be rushed.

If they're not ready to talk now, they probably will be — as long as they feel respected.

You're not interrogating; you're inviting.

And the more comfortable they feel, the more honest their answers become.

The Catch & Release Method
Ask with warmth.
Listen without interrupting.
Release pressure and revisit naturally.
Sales is a conversation, not a courtroom.

The Magic of Summarizing

Once you've asked your questions and listened deeply, finish discovery with a simple summary:

"So, if I'm hearing you right, you're looking for a home that gives you more space for the kids — each with their own bathroom, a backyard that fits a pool and space for the dog, a kitchen that lets you host big get-togethers, a media room, a game room, and still keeps you within 20 minutes of work. Is that right? Anything I'm missing?"

This small step is powerful. It proves you were listening — and gives them the chance to confirm or correct what matters most.

When people feel understood, they're ready to be guided.

Pro Tip:
Buyers trust who understands them most — not who talks the most.

Closing Reflection

Great questions don't just reveal information — they reveal emotion.

They create clarity where confusion lived, and confidence where hesitation used to be.

Ask questions constantly — even during your presentation.

When you're showing a home with different features, use micro-questions to keep discovery going:

"This home has the sink in the island, but the next one doesn't — do you prefer it this way?"

"Does that matter to you, or do you like it better on the wall?"

These quick check-ins keep buyers engaged and help you fine-tune what truly matters to them.

When you master the art of asking, you'll never have to chase buyers — they'll start chasing you.

Because when people feel heard, they follow.

_____

_____

_____

_____

_____

_____

_____

_____

_____

_____

_____

_____

_____

_____

_____

_____

_____

_____

_____

_____

_____

_____

_____

_____

_____

_____

5

READING THE BUYER
UNDERSTAND WHAT BUYERS
SAY WITHOUT WORDS

Every buyer communicates differently — some through words, some through tone, and many through body language. You've learned to ask great questions; now let's explore how to listen beyond words. The best sales professionals don't just *hear* what's being said — they *read* what's happening underneath.

Understanding buyer signals is one of the most powerful skills you can develop.

When you can interpret hesitation, interest, or doubt without a word being spoken, you gain the ability to guide the conversation with confidence and empathy.

Body language often reveals the Truth before words can catch up.

· Leaning in = interest.

· Crossed arms = discomfort or skepticism.

· Nodding or mirroring your movement = trust.

· Glancing repeatedly at a partner = indecision.

You don't need to become a behavioral expert, but learning to read these small cues helps you adapt naturally in real time.

If you'd like to go deeper on this topic, books such as *What Every BODY Is Saying* by Joe Navarro or *The Like Switch* by Jack Schafer offer incredible insight into reading human behavior.

> **Pro Tip:**
> Buyers rarely say exactly what they mean — but they always *show* it.

Listening to Learn, Not to Respond

When you're showing a home, your job isn't to talk the buyer into something. It's to *listen* your way toward the right fit.

I make it a personal rule that the buyer should talk at least 60% of the time during a tour.

That doesn't mean you're silent — it means you're asking great questions and then listening *with intention.*

Active listening is more than hearing words. It's noticing pauses, tone, and energy shifts.

When someone's excitement fades halfway through a tour, that's a cue.

When their eyes light up in the kitchen, or they slow down in the backyard, that's data you can use.

Every sigh, smile, and side glance tells a story — if you're paying attention.

> ### The 3 Levels of Listening
> **Hearing:** The words they say.
> **Interpreting:** The meaning behind them.
> **Feeling:** The emotion driving them.
> **Master level** = listening to all three at once.

Handling Negative Reactions

Negative reactions aren't deal killers — they're guideposts.

When a buyer says, "I hate this kitchen," don't defend it. Explore it.

Ask:

"What about it isn't working for you?"

If they struggle to explain, help them narrow it down:

"Is it the layout, the color, or maybe the size of the island?"

This shows curiosity instead of defensiveness — and it helps you uncover what they truly value.

Sometimes, the issue isn't even the kitchen. It's something emotional, like:

"My mom's kitchen was always open — this feels too closed off."

You can gently connect it back:

"How does this compare to your current kitchen? What would you change if you could?"

The key is to never take negative feedback personally. Use it as a compass that points you closer to their "yes."

> **Pro Tip:**
> Every "no" gets you closer to what they'll say "yes" to —
> if you're listening.

When the Buyer Is Quiet

Not everyone expresses enthusiasm out loud. Some buyers need time to observe and think.

If you push too hard during that silence, you risk breaking their trust.

When I sense a quiet buyer, I slow down and shift to a personal topic — something like,

"What do you all enjoy doing on weekends?"

or

"How's the new home shopping process been so far?"

That small pivot resets the energy and gives them a chance to relax.

Once they feel more comfortable, they'll open up again about the home.

Sometimes the best thing you can do is give space — and let silence do the selling.

The Power of Silence
Silence makes people think.
Don't rush to fill it.
The moment you stop talking, the buyer starts processing — and that's when decisions form.

Navigating Price Objections

Price objections are almost universal — and they're rarely about the price itself.

They're about *perceived value.*

When a buyer says, *"That's too high,"* I don't argue. I explore.

"I totally understand. Help me out — what were you hoping this home would be priced at?"

Or

"What price point are you trying to stay near?"

Now you're not defending; you're discovering.

Maybe they saw something cheaper online. Maybe they're comparing communities and/or another builder.

Once you understand their reference point, you can realign value through benefits, not discounts.

> **✓ Reframe the Price**
> Price ≠ Problem.
> Price = Opportunity to show value.

Sometimes, I separate the conversation from total price and shift to monthly payment.

For many buyers, it's not about the total — it's about what fits comfortably into their life.

"If this home fits everything you're looking for, and we can keep the payment within your comfort zone, would it make sense to move forward?"

That question transitions the conversation from price anxiety to possibility.

This is worth repeating: get a mortgage calculator from your preferred lender and learn how to use it confidently.

It builds instant credibility and helps buyers understand the real numbers behind their purchase.

Helping Buyers Choose Between Two Favorites

When a buyer says, "We love both homes — we just can't decide," that's a great problem to have.

It means they're emotionally ready — now they just need clarity.

This is where your skill as a guide comes in.

Ask them to compare priorities:

"Which feature feels more important — the larger kitchen or the extra bedroom?"

"Which one feels more like home when you picture your family there?"

"If one of these disappeared from the market tomorrow, which would you regret missing most?"

Then, get quiet. Let them talk it out.

You're not deciding for them — you're helping them discover their decision.

Pro Tip:
Never take sides between partners — be the neutral guide who helps them find common ground.

Closing the Showing with Confidence

As the tour wraps up, I like to end with an open, easygoing question:

"So, did we find the right home today?"

If the answer is no, I want to understand what's holding them back. So, I'll follow up with: "Thank you for sharing. If you don't mind me asking, is there something specific that's missing, like a feature, or is it something else?"

That feedback shapes what I show next — and shows the buyer I'm committed to *their* goals, not my quota.

If the answer is yes, I reinforce it confidently:

"That's great — I had a feeling this one might be the one."

That simple line transfers belief — and belief often becomes action.

If you saw a few different homes, you can ask something like:

"Which of the homes we saw today feels closest to what you're looking for?"

This answer will help guide you to the one if you haven't already found it.

 The Post-Tour Framework
Ask for clarity ("Did we find the right home?")
Adjust next steps based on feedback.
Reinforce positive emotion.
Every showing ends with direction — forward, not flat.

Closing Reflection

Reading buyers isn't about manipulation — it's about empathy.

It's seeing beyond words to understand what people truly mean.

When you can tune into tone, timing, and emotion, you stop chasing sales — and start leading them.

Every home tells a story, and every buyer speaks a language.

Learn to read both, and you'll never lose your place in the conversation again.

_____

_____

_____

_____

_____

_____

_____

_____

_____

_____

_____

_____

_____

_____

_____

_____

_____

_____

_____

6

RECOGNIZING BUYING SIGNALS AND GUIDING THE DECISION

The best closers don't force decisions — they recognize them

Most buyers won't say, *"We're ready to buy."* Instead, they drop subtle clues through their questions, tone, and behavior.

Your job is to catch those signals early and help the buyer take the next step with clarity and confidence.

> **Pro Tip:**
> You don't *create* buying moments — you *notice* them.

Recognizing Buying Signals

Buying signals come in three forms — **verbal, emotional, and behavioral.**

Learning to read all three is what turns a good salesperson into a trusted advisor.

Type	What it sounds/Looks Like	What it Means
Verbal	"Would our couch fit here? / "What are the next steps?"	They're picturing ownership.
Emotional	Smiling, slowing down, or showing concern about losing it	They're emotionally invested.
Behavioral	Taking measurements, revisiting rooms, asking contract details	They're mentally committing.

When a buyer starts imagining or *visualizing* their life inside the home, the decision is already 80% made.

They're no longer browsing — they're *bonding.*

> ### ▌ The "Imagine Test"
> When a buyer says, *"Imagine the kids running down these stairs…"* — that's not small talk.
> That's ownership language.
> Follow that spark — it's your window to close.

Soft Closes Throughout the Tour

Closing doesn't happen at the end of a tour — it happens *throughout* it.

Each small "yes" you gather builds momentum toward the final one.

I like to sprinkle soft closes during tours, such as:

- "Does this kitchen feel like what you had in mind?"
- "How does this layout compare to what you've seen so far?"
- "Could you see this working for your family's routine?"

These questions create micro-agreements. By the time you ask for the big yes, they've already said yes a dozen smaller times.

> **Pro Tip:**
> Soft closes aren't tricks — they're trust checkpoints.

When to Move Toward the Close

Almost every successful appointment has a moment when energy shifts. The buyer stops exploring and starts imagining. Their tone changes, they linger longer, they start picturing furniture or family gatherings. They will start asking each other questions like, "Where would we put the Christmas tree?"

That's your cue.

You don't need a dramatic close — just confident, calm guidance.

Here are a few examples that work well:

- "It seems like this one really checks the boxes for you — are you ready to take it off the market before someone else does?"
- "You mentioned this feels right for your family; do you want to go ahead and take the next step?"
- "Would you like me to see if we can get this exact home reserved for you today?"

Each option is assumptive but warm — framed as help, not pressure.

> ### ⊘ The Three-Step Close
> Identify: Notice readiness cues.
> Confirm: Ask gentle verification questions ("Does this feel like the one?").
> Guide: Offer next steps naturally ("Let's secure it so it doesn't get away.").

Handling Hesitation with Empathy

Even when a buyer loves a home, hesitation is normal. Doubt creeps in. Fear of overcommitting or making a mistake can momentarily freeze decision-making. Second-guessing and financial stress can all surface in the final moments.

When someone says, *"We just need to think about it,"* never argue — explore.

Say something like:

"I completely understand — this is a big decision. What would help you feel more confident tonight?"

Or:

"Is there something specific you'd like to sleep on, or just wanting to take a breather?"

Both options invite honesty and uncover what's really causing the pause. Sometimes it's timing; sometimes it's uncertainty about financing, or sometimes it's the lot. Whatever the case, empathy keeps the conversation open. You're showing that you care about their comfort more than your commission — and that earns respect.

 Pro Tip:
Empathy doesn't slow down the sale — it *saves* it.

REAL-LIFE EXAMPLE:

The Couple Who "Needed to Think"

I once worked with a couple who were visibly in love with a home but said they needed time to "talk things over." Instead of pushing, I said:

"Absolutely — you should. Why don't I hold this one for 48 hours so it doesn't get taken while you're deciding?"

They called the next morning, ready to move forward. What they really needed wasn't time — it was permission to breathe.

The 48-Hour Hold

A 48-hour hold is one of my favorite strategies in slower markets or with hesitant buyers — **but only when your leadership supports it.**

You can say:

"Why don't we secure the home with a small deposit so it's off the market for 48 hours? That way, you've got peace of mind that no one else can take it, and you can make sure it feels right."

This approach turns pressure into protection. And once the home is held — most never back out once the decision settles overnight.

> ↙ **Fear vs. Regret**
> Buyers aren't afraid of buying.
> They're afraid of *regretting* buying.
> Your job is to replace fear with *confidence*.

Dealing With Buyer's Remorse

Even after signing, buyers sometimes feel uneasy.

That's normal — it's called *post-decision dissonance.* Most of us know it as *Buyer's Remorse.*

When you sense it, don't avoid it — address it head-on.

Reaffirm their decision by revisiting what mattered to them:

"You mentioned this lot being perfect for your morning walks and the kitchen layout fitting your family's needs — those things haven't changed."

By revisiting *their* words, you reaffirm that their choice was sound.

It's not about re-selling the home; it's about re-centering the buyer. Reassurance keeps excitement alive long after the contract ink dries.

 The Reassurance Loop
Revisit their motivation.
Reconfirm their excitement.
Reframe their decision as wise, not rushed.

Knowing When to Step Back

The best closers know when to pause.

If one partner is ready and the other isn't, take the side of caution. You will build far more trust this way.

I'll often say:

"Why don't we regroup this weekend and make sure it feels right for both of you? I want both of you to feel completely comfortable."

Sometimes, the pause is the close. That kind of patience builds trust — and trust turns into long-term business.

Pro Tip:
A confident pause can be more persuasive than another pitch.

Following Up After the Appointment

How you follow up after the appointment says everything about your professionalism.

If they didn't buy, your tone should stay consistent — calm, caring, and respectful; not desperate.

A simple message like:

"Hi [Name], it was great meeting you today! I know there's a lot to think through, but I just wanted to say I really enjoyed our visit. I'm here if any new questions come up."

Or, for someone who's close but undecided:

"I know you wanted to talk things over — totally understand. I'll keep an eye on the home and let you know if anything changes. I'm here if you want to run through any numbers or ideas."

That small, thoughtful touch separates you from everyone else they met that week.

---

17 The 24-Hour Rule

Follow up within 24 hours, always.
Strike while the memory — and the emotion — is still fresh.

Closing Reflection

Recognizing buying signals is about *reading readiness,* not *creating pressure.*

It's about aligning with the buyer's pace, guiding with empathy, and helping them make a confident decision that feels like *their own.*

Every "yes" you earn along the way — each small agreement, each moment of clarity — leads to the big one naturally.

That's the beauty of trust-based selling.

When your process is steady, and your heart's in the right place, you'll never have to push for a close — you'll simply guide buyers into it.

_____

_____

_____

_____

7

BUILDING LONG-TERM RELATIONSHIPS AND REFERRAL BUSINESS

A closing isn't the end of the relationship — it's the beginning of the next one.

Every contract you write is a chance to create a client for life, and every homeowner you serve can become an advocate who sells your next three homes for you.

The best new home sales professionals don't chase volume — they cultivate loyalty.

They know that when you treat people right *after* the sale, they remember you *before* their next one.

> **Pro Tip:**
> Referrals aren't earned with discounts — they're earned with dependability.

Maintaining Contact After Closing

Most salespeople vanish after the handshake.

But that's exactly when trust has the most power — when the buyer is now a homeowner, adjusting to their new space and sharing their story with friends.

I make it a habit to reach out three times after every closing:

- **30 days:** "Just checking in — how's the move going?"
- **90 days:** "Have you discovered your favorite spot in the house yet?"
- **1 year:** "Happy home anniversary!"

These quick touchpoints don't take long, but they can mean *everything* to the homeowner.

They show that your care didn't end at closing — it simply shifted form.

> **The 3 Touch Framework**
> **Appreciate:** Thank them for trusting you.
> **Reconnect:** Check on their experience.
> **Reinforce:** Remind them you're always here as a resource.

Making the Follow-Up Genuine

Follow-up is only powerful if it feels personal.

Buyers can tell when you're checking a box versus when you truly care.

That's why I always personalize my outreach.

Instead of sending a generic "thank you," I'll say:

"Hey [Name], I was thinking about your family the other day — did your son end up picking his room with the bigger closet?"

It's small details like that which remind people that you *listened.*

You can't fake authenticity.

When your follow-up comes from genuine care, referrals happen naturally — you won't even have to ask.

Pro Tip:
People refer to the professional who made them *feel seen.*

When and How to Introduce Referrals

You don't need to beg for referrals — you just need to *invite* them.

Timing is everything.

I never bring up referrals during the stress of the buying process.

Instead, I wait until the end — once they've closed and are genuinely happy.

I'll say something like:

"It's been such a pleasure helping you with this home. If you ever have friends or family who are thinking about building nearby — or who'd love to live down the street from you — send them my way. I'd love to take care of them the same way."

It's light, friendly, and memorable.

You're not selling — you're extending gratitude.

🏠 The Referral Moment

The best time to ask for a referral is when your buyer is *smiling*.

Best Practices for Referral Outreach

Different people respond to different styles of contact.

Younger homeowners prefer texts or DMs.

Older clients value a phone call or handwritten note.

If I know a homeowner has referred someone, I immediately reach out with thanks — even before the referral turns into a sale.

Something like:

"I just heard from your friend [Name] — thank you so much for connecting us! It means a lot that you thought of me."

Then, if the referral closes, I'll follow up again — this time with a thank-you card or small gift card.

Consistency in appreciation creates consistency in referrals.

Pro Tip:
Referrals are a reflection of *trust, not timing*. Keep earning both.

Managing Referrals Professionally

When someone introduces you to a friend or family member, treat that relationship like gold.

You're not just representing yourself — you're representing the trust the referrer placed in you.

Whenever possible, I prefer direct introductions (group text or email).

It creates an instant bridge of trust and allows you to acknowledge both parties.

And always close the loop:

"Thank you again for the introduction! I'll take great care of them."

That reassurance strengthens both relationships — the new lead and the existing client.

 The Trust Chain
When a past client refers someone, your professionalism affects *both* relationships.
Honor both ends of the chain.

Leveraging CRM and Systems

Referrals grow when you stay consistent — and consistency comes from systems.

I use my CRM to track every buyer, follow-up date, and referral opportunity.

Each month, I set reminders for "check-in weeks" — short bursts of outreach that keep me top of mind without feeling robotic.

If your CRM allows automation, use it for reminders — but never for your messages.

Authenticity can't be automated.

---

17 The 30-90-360 Rule
Reach out 30 days, 90 days, and 1 year after closing.
It's not just follow-up — it's follow-through.
Consistency builds trust, and trust builds referrals.

Keeping Gratitude Personal

When someone sends you a referral, say thank you *immediately*.

Not with a script — with sincerity.

A quick text works fine:

"You just made my day — thank you so much for the referral! I'll make sure they're taken care of."

And if the referral turns into a sale, show tangible appreciation.

Send a handwritten card. Deliver a small gift.

You don't need to go big — you just need to go *genuine*.

Gratitude is the most underused marketing tool in sales.

Pro Tip:
A heartfelt thank-you is worth more than any incentive program.

Turning Relationships Into Legacy

When you treat every client like a long-term friend instead of a transaction, something powerful happens — your business compounds.

Each family you serve becomes part of your story.

Their trust becomes your reputation.

After enough years, your success won't come from chasing new leads — it'll come from *past clients sending future ones.*

That's not luck. That's loyalty — built intentionally, one relationship at a time.

The Relationship Flywheel

Serve with excellence.
Follow up with care.
Show gratitude consistently.
Watch referrals create momentum.

Closing Reflection

Referrals don't come from transactions — they come from *trust.*

And trust is built by doing small things exceptionally well, long after the sale is over.

When you lead with gratitude, follow through with consistency, and genuinely care about the families you serve, you'll never have to chase business again — it will come to you.

Because people may forget the square footage or the upgrade list,

but they'll never forget how you made them feel.

That's the legacy of a true sales professional.

_____

_____

_____

_____

_____

_____

_____

_____

_____

_____

_____

_____

_____

_____

_____

_____

_____

_____

_____

_____

_____

_____

✎ Next Steps

- Which relationship-building habit will you implement first?

_____

_____

_____

- How will you personalize your 30-90-360 follow-up rhythm?

_____

_____

_____

- Who can you thank today for a past referral?

_____

_____

_____

ABOUT THE AUTHOR

Ryan Roten has spent nearly two decades helping families navigate one of the most meaningful decisions of their lives: buying a home. As a New Home Sales Counselor with Highland Homes in the Dallas–Fort Worth area, Ryan has built a reputation for his relationship-driven approach to sales — one rooted in listening, clarity, and genuine service rather than pressure or scripts.

Over the course of his career, Ryan has worked with thousands of buyers and real estate professionals, learning firsthand that great salespeople succeed not because they talk the most, but because they understand people the best. His approach centers on asking thoughtful questions, reading the buyer's energy, and creating an experience built on trust and transparency.

Ryan's philosophy has been shaped not only by years in the field, but by his commitment to personal growth, consistency, and faith-grounded principles. He believes the best careers are built through steady habits, resilience during market shifts, and a genuine desire to help others succeed.

Ryan lives in North Texas with his wife, Vanessa, and their six children. When he's not helping buyers find the right home, he enjoys spending time with family, investing in personal growth, and encouraging other sales professionals to build careers based on clarity, connection, and long-term relationships.

RyanRoten.com

TRAININGS AND TOOLS
THAT CREATE CLARITY

Thank you for reading *Questions That Create Clarity*.

My hope is that this book encourages you to approach sales with greater clarity, confidence, and connection.

While my primary focus remains helping buyers and Realtors in the field each day, I always enjoy connecting with other sales professionals who are committed to improving their craft.

If you'd like to share your thoughts about the book, ask a question, or simply say hello, you're welcome to reach out.

Ryan@ryanroten.com

RyanRoten.com

From time to time, I may also offer coaching conversations or team discussions around the ideas in this book.

Wherever your career takes you, remember that the best sales professionals don't rely on pressure — they rely on clarity, consistency, and genuine connection.

ACKNOWLEDGMENTS

No meaningful work is accomplished alone, and this book is no exception.

First and foremost, I want to thank my wife, Vanessa, and our children for their constant encouragement and support. Writing a book takes time, focus, and patience, and their belief in me made the journey possible.

I'm also grateful to the many mentors, leaders, and colleagues I've worked alongside throughout my career in new home sales. Each conversation, challenge, and shared experience has helped shape the lessons found in these pages.

A special thank you to the real estate professionals and buyers I've had the privilege of working with over the years. Your questions, perspectives, and trust have taught me far more than any sales manual ever could.

And finally, thank you to everyone who encouraged this project along the way and helped bring it to life.

APPENDIX
THE CONSTRUCTION GLOSSARY:

Terms Every New Home Professional Should Know

Appraisal:
An estimate of a property's value completed by a professional appraiser.

Blueprint:
A scaled drawing that shows the design and layout of a home — used for planning, pricing, and permitting.

Block:
A group of continuous lots on a plat map.

Build Job (Dirt Sale):
A home sold before construction begins.

Building Codes:
Local or state regulations that define how homes must be constructed for safety and quality.

Bust:
When a sales contract is canceled by the buyer.

Certificate of Occupancy (CO):
Issued by the city or county once all inspections are complete and the home meets code requirements. The home cannot be occupied until this certificate is granted.

Change Order (CO):
A written document used to modify a sales agreement or construction plan — for adding or removing options, price changes, or discretionary discounts.

Closing:
The final step in a real estate transaction when ownership transfers to the buyer.

Closing Disclosure (CD):
A standardized form from the lender that provides the final details of the mortgage, including loan terms, monthly payment, and closing costs.

Comps (Comparable Sales):
Recently sold homes used by appraisers to determine property value.

Contingency Agreement:
A contract that allows buyers time to sell their current home before purchasing a new one.

Deed:
The legal document that transfers ownership of the property.

Earnest Money (Deposit):
Funds given by the buyer when signing a contract to show good faith. May be refundable or non-refundable depending on contract terms.

Elevation:
A drawing of the exterior of a home showing materials, roof pitch, and architectural details.

Floor Plan:
A bird's-eye view showing the home's room layout, dimensions, and overall flow.

HERS Index:
The Home Energy Rating System score. Lower scores mean higher energy efficiency.

Homeowners Association (HOA):
A governing body that maintains community standards and amenities. Homeowners pay dues for upkeep and shared benefits.

Job Number:
A six-digit code identifying a specific home and lot — the first three digits indicate the community, and the last three refer to the homesite.

Lot:
The homesite or parcel of land where a home is built.

Lot Fit:
A plan overlay showing how a specific home fits on a specific lot, accounting for easements and setbacks.

Lot Premium:
An added (or discounted) cost for a lot based on its location, size, or features such as greenbelt or cul-de-sac positioning.

Model Home:
A home built to showcase a builder's product and features. Often remains open for tours during sales.

Permit:
A legal document issued by the local jurisdiction allowing construction to begin.

Phase / Section:
A portion of a community released for building. Some neighborhoods are built in multiple phases.

Plan:
The chosen architectural design or floor plan for a home.

Plat Map:
An aerial map showing property boundaries, lot numbers, and community layout.

Plot Plan:
A scaled drawing showing the placement of the home on the lot, including setbacks, easements, and legal descriptions.

Pre-approval:
A lender's verification that a buyer qualifies for a mortgage up to a specific amount based on verified income, assets, and credit.

Pre-qualification:
An estimate of borrowing capacity based on self-reported financial information.

Product Width / Product Line:
Refers to the home series and lot size — for example, a 40' product is built on a 50' lot.

Punch List:
A list of final construction items that must be completed or corrected before closing.

Purchase Order (PO):
A document confirming the purchase of goods or services from a vendor at an agreed price.

Sales Agreement / Contract:
The legal agreement between builder and buyer outlining the home purchase terms.

Sales Worksheet:
An internal form used to track profit details after a sale.

SAM:
Construction scheduling software used to manage home builds.

Spec (Inventory Home):
A "speculative" home started before it's sold. It may be complete or still customizable.

Standard Specs:
The list of features and materials included in a home at no extra cost.

Start Date:
The date construction officially begins.

Subdivision / Community:
A neighborhood development made up of multiple lots, product lines, or project numbers.

Swing:
Indicates which side of the home the garage is located on (left swing or right swing).

Title Company:
Handles ownership verification and ensures the property can transfer without legal issues.

Transfer:
When a buyer switches from one homesite or home to another within the same community.

Walkthrough (Final Walk):
The buyer's final inspection before closing to ensure all items are complete and satisfactory.

Common Acronyms
CD – Closing Disclosure
CO – Change Order / Certificate of Occupancy (context matters)
CM – Construction Manager
ECDA – Estimated Closing Date Addendum
HERS – Home Energy Rating System
MLS – Multiple Listing Service
P&H – Permit and Hold
PM – Project Manager
PO – Purchase Order
SAM – Scheduling Application for Management
TREC – Texas Real Estate Commission

RyanRoten.com

www.ingramcontent.com/pod-product-compliance
Lightning Source LLC
Chambersburg PA
CBHW070433290526
45791CB00005B/1950